MW00777659

How To Tap Dance By Nick Castle, Hollywood's Foremost Dance Director And Teacher Of The Stars

Nick Castle

Introduction

The booklet you are about to study is designed to teach you the basic steps in the art of TAP DANCING. As simple as it may look, it is the result of many months of extensive study and research. I have endeavored to embrace all the fundamentals of TAP in such a manner as to enable the beginner to understand and master that type of dance.

In order for this book to do the job for which it is intended, you, as the student, must be **willing to learn and work hard.** Develop your own practice plan — either rehearse alone or with someone, you'll discover it to be healthy exercise besides fun and entertainment for others as well as yourself.

Always keep in mind the importance of the **FIRST FIVE BASIC STEPS** — they are the foundation or groundwork in learning to Tap — master them and you will have no difficulty with the other steps, since all Tap steps invariably consist of the **FIRST FIVE BASIC STEPS** in various combinations.

One last bit of advice—**DON'T** try to conquer the ART of TAP overnight. Read and understand the instructions before attempting to do the steps, study the illustrations, practice long and hard, maintain a "don't give up" attitude and believe me, you will succeed in learning to Tap . . . Well, let's go to work now . . . Have fun and Good Luck with "Happy Taps".

Nick Castle.

The author wishes to thank Miss Juanita Marie Arno and Messrs. Charles O'Curran and Michael Clemens for their help in making this book possible.

MUSICAL TERMS

1. RHYTHM—
Keeping in strict time with the music.

2. COUNTING—
Important term in TAP DANCING, used to give the musical time to each step.
(A) WALTZ—MUSIC 3/4 TEMPO
3 counts to one measure or bar of music.
(B) FOX TROT—MUSIC 4/4 TEMPO
4 counts to one measure or bar of music.
(C) FAST FOX TROT—MUSIC 2/4 TEMPO
2 counts to one measure or bar of music.

3. TEMPO—
Counting the musical time of each step.

DEFINITIONS

BREAK—Used at the end of a dance step.

HOP—To spring up and land on same foot. No transfer of weight. (ONE SOUND)

JUMP—A leap from one foot to the other in any direction. (ONE SOUND)

LUNGE—To stamp foot forward, or in any direction, with knee bent. (ONE SOUND)

SCRAPE—To drag or bring foot to a closed position, (ONE MOVEMENT)

SLIDE—Opposite of Scrape—to push the foot on floor in any direction (ONE MOVEMENT)

STAMP—Like a step, but heavier with weight on flat of the foot. May be taken without transfer of weight. (ONE SOUND)

STEP—The transfer of weight from one foot to the other. (ONE SOUND)

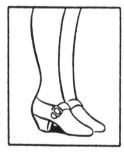 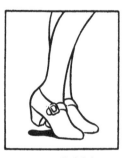 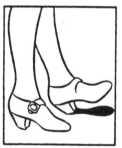 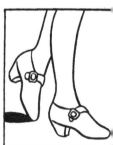

| **FLAT** | **BALL** | **HEEL** | **TOE** |

FOOT POSITIONS AND THEIR **TAP SOUNDS**

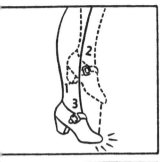

NICK CASTLE'S MODERN TAP TECHNIQUE

1. THE SINGLE TAP.

Raise RIGHT foot off floor then step on ball of RIGHT foot. (one sound)
REPEAT ON LEFT FOOT.

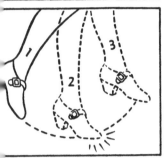

2. THE BRUSH.

Hit ball of RIGHT foot while swinging it forward (one sound). (May be taken in any direction)
REPEAT ON LEFT FOOT.

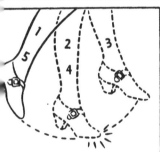

3. THE SHUFFLE.

Brush the ball of the RIGHT foot forward and back. (two sounds)
REPEAT ON LEFT FOOT.

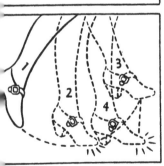

4. FLAP OR DOUBLE TAP.

Brush the ball of the RIGHT foot forward then step on RIGHT foot. (two sounds)
REPEAT ON LEFT FOOT.

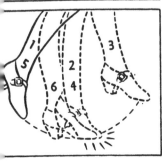

5. THE TRIPLE TAP. (Shuffle Step)

Brush the RIGHT foot forward, brush the RIGHT foot back, then step on ball of RIGHT foot. (three sounds)
REPEAT ON LEFT FOOT.

Important! Know the first five steps before proceeding.

6. CHUG.
Bend the knees and straighten knees sliding backwards. May be done on both feet or on right or left foot. (two movements)

7. PATTER.
Fast steps taken (in place) on the balls of alternating feet. (four or more sounds)

8. SINGLE TAP NERVE.
Trembling the leg, tapping the floor with the ball of the foot.

9. BALL CHANGE.
Two quick steps taken on the balls of both feet changing weight from RIGHT to LEFT (two sounds)

10. IRISH.
A shuffle-hop-step. Taken in place, moving forward or back or crossing. (four sounds)

11. TOE TAP.
Hitting tip of RIGHT toe in back of LEFT foot. (one sound)
REPEAT ON LEFT FOOT.

12. TOE STRUT.
A style of walking. Start with RIGHT toe in back of LEFT heel. Toe Tap on RIGHT, drop LEFT heel, step forward on RIGHT foot. (three sounds)
REPEAT ON LEFT FOOT.

13. DIG HEEL.
Step forward on ball of RIGHT foot, then drop RIGHT heel. (two sounds)
REPEAT ON LEFT FOOT.

14. FLAP HEEL.
Flap RIGHT foot dropping the RIGHT heel. (three sounds)
REPEAT ON LEFT FOOT.

15. TRIPLE HEEL.
Shuffle-step (in place) on RIGHT foot dropping RIGHT heel. (four sounds)
REPEAT ON LEFT FOOT.

16. QUINT TAP.
Shuffle-step (in place) on RIGHT foot, drop RIGHT heel then stamp LEFT foot. (five sounds)
REPEAT ON LEFT FOOT.

17. HEEL TAP.
Hit heel of RIGHT FOOT IN ANY DIRECTION. (one sound)
REPEAT ON LEFT FOOT.

18. HEEL SCUFF.
Like a brush but using the heel instead of the ball of the foot. (one sound)

19. HEEL TWIST.
Place RIGHT foot flat on floor. Raise the toe from the floor and turn the toe inward or outward. (one movement)
REPEAT ON LEFT FOOT.

20. HEEL CHANGE.
Place heel of RIGHT foot forward then step back on ball of LEFT foot. (two sounds)

21. HEEL ROLL.
Raise RIGHT heel, drop RIGHT heel. Raise LEFT heel, drop LEFT heel. REPEAT THESE HEEL BEATS. (four sounds). Practice for speed.

22. CRAMP ROLL.
Single tap on ball of RIGHT foot. Single tap on ball of LEFT foot. Drop RIGHT heel, then drop LEFT heel. (four sounds)
REPEAT ON LEFT FOOT.

23. NERVE ROLL.
Two shuffles on RIGHT foot. (four sounds). Practice for speed.
REPEAT ON LEFT FOOT.

24. CASTLE ROLL.
Two fast shuffles on RIGHT foot, then drop LEFT heel. (five sounds)
REPEAT ON LEFT FOOT.

25. PEARL ROLLS.
(A) SINGLE.
Single tap on ball of RIGHT foot, shuffle LEFT foot, drop RIGHT heel.
(B) DOUBLE.
Flap on ball of RIGHT foot, shuffle LEFT foot, drop RIGHT heel.
(C) TRIPLE.
Triple tap on ball of RIGHT foot, shuffle LEFT foot, drop RIGHT heel.
(A) Four sounds, (B) Five sounds, (C) Six sounds
REPEAT ON LEFT FOOT.

26. DRUM ROLLS.
Shuffle RIGHT, hop on LEFT foot, then flap on RIGHT foot. (five sounds)
REPEAT ON LEFT FOOT.

27. BACK FLAP.
Same as FLAP only brushing the RIGHT foot backwards, then stepping down on the RIGHT foot. (two sounds)
REPEAT ON LEFT FOOT.

28. HOLLYWOOD ROLLS.
Heel tap on RIGHT foot, back flap on RIGHT foot, then drop the RIGHT heel. (four fast sounds)
REPEAT ON LEFT FOOT.

29. MILITARY FLAPS.
Double flaps done fast, alternating on RIGHT and LEFT foot.
REPEAT STARTING LEFT FOOT.

30. PICK-UP.
Stand on RIGHT foot (LEFT foot raised), brush RIGHT back, ending on ball of RIGHT foot. (two sounds)
REPEAT ON LEFT FOOT.

31. PULL BACK.
Raise LEFT foot off floor. Then slide RIGHT foot backwards of floor. (one sound)
REPEAT ON LEFT FOOT.

32. BUFFALO.
Step down on RIGHT to side. Shuffle the LEFT foot from a side position, then cross the LEFT foot in back of the RIGHT foot, stepping on it, at the same time lifting the RIGHT foot in front of LEFT ankle. This step usually taken moving to side, right or left. (four sounds)
REPEAT STARTING LEFT FOOT.

33. BELLS.
Stand with the weight on LEFT foot, RIGHT foot extended to side. Jump up striking the heel of the RIGHT foot against the heel of the LEFT foot. Finish in starting position. (one sound)
REPEAT ON LEFT FOOT.

34. FALLING-OFF-THE-LOG.

Hold RIGHT leg to side, jump down on the RIGHT while kicking the LEFT in front of RIGHT leg. Jump down on LEFT kicking RIGHT to side. Jump across in front of LEFT foot with RIGHT bending LEFT knee in back of RIGHT.

REPEAT ON LEFT FOOT.

35. BOMBERSHAY.

Step on RIGHT foot to right side, heel-twist on LEFT outwards, then back flap LEFT. Repeat, moving to right side. (three sounds)

REPEAT ON LEFT FOOT.

36. MAXIE.

Jump on RIGHT foot, shuffle the LEFT forward, pick up with the RIGHT, finishing with a step on the LEFT FOOT. (five sounds).

REPEAT ON LEFT FOOT.

37. WALTZ CLOG.

(A) SINGLE TAP WALTZ CLOG.

Single tap on RIGHT foot, shuffle on the LEFT foot, then ball change from LEFT to RIGHT. (five sounds)

(B) DOUBLE TAP WALTZ CLOG.

Begin with DOUBLE TAP on RIGHT foot. (six sounds)

REPEAT ON LEFT FOOT.

38. RIFFS.

(A) 4 TAP RIFF.

Hit tip of RIGHT toe, then heel of RIGHT as foot is brushed forward, place the RIGHT heel on floor, then drop the RIGHT toe. (four sounds)

(B) 5 TAP RIFF.

Add heel tap on the LEFT after first toe heel sounds. (five sounds)

(C) 6 TAP RIFF.

Add heel on the RIGHT foot at end of 5 tap riff. (six sounds)

REPEAT EACH ON LEFT FOOT.

39. ANKLE TURN.

Complete turn made on the ball of the RIGHT foot, lifting the LEFT foot in back of the RIGHT ankle.
REPEAT ON LEFT FOOT.

40. PADDLE TURNS.

Step to RIGHT on the RIGHT foot, brush LEFT forward, ball change LEFT to RIGHT. Then ankle turn to RIGHT—ending front with left stamp.
REPEAT ON LEFT FOOT.

41. PIVOT TURNS.

Complete turn made on one or both feet by raising the heel or heels off the floor.
REPEAT TURNING RIGHT OR LEFT.

42. THREE STEP TURN.

Step on RIGHT foot to RIGHT side, step on LEFT foot crossing LEFT over the RIGHT pivoting on the RIGHT foot making a half turn RIGHT. Swing the RIGHT foot around pivoting on the ball of the LEFT foot, then step down on the RIGHT foot to side completing the turn.
REPEAT ON LEFT FOOT.

Movie Stars
Famous Tap Dance Steps

The following dance steps are typical of the characteristic style of these movie stars. The steps are arranged to fit eight measures of music.

BILL ROBINSON STEP

Begin RIGHT foot. Shuffle R. Hop L. Shuffle step back on RIGHT. Back flap LEFT to meet RIGHT. Shuffle R. Hop L. Cross RIGHT over LEFT (IRISH) stepping on RIGHT. Drop RIGHT heel. Toe tap LEFT to side (on toe tap look over LEFT shoulder. (Ct. & a 1 & a 2 & 3 & 4 & 5 6 7) 2 MEAS. REPEAT ON LEFT FOOT THEN
AGAIN ON RIGHT..4 MEAS.

BREAK:

Shuffle LEFT, hop RIGHT, step on LEFT, triple tap on RIGHT, shuffle LEFT, hop RIGHT, Flap on LEFT, Flap on RIGHT. (Ct. & a 1 2 & 3 & 4 & 5 & 6 & 7)............2 MEAS.
8 MEAS.

Music Suggestion: Melody in "F"

ANN MILLER STEP

Stamp forward on RIGHT. (No weight.)
Stamp forward on RIGHT. (Weight on RIGHT.)
Step back on ball of LEFT foot, brush the RIGHT back, drop LEFT heel, step back on ball o fRIGHT foot, brush the LEFT back, drop RIGHT heel, step back on LEFT foot. Back flap RIGHT. (Ct. 1 2 3 & 4 & 5 & 6 & 7)....2 MEAS.

Shuffle LEFT, drop RIGHT heel, step back on LEFT.
Stamp forward on RIGHT, Stamp forward on LEFT in place, Brush the RIGHT back, drop the LEFT heel, step back on RIGHT foot, brush the LEFT back, drop the RIGHT heel, step back on LEFT foot, Stamp forward on RIGHT, Stamp forward on left.
(Ct. & 8 & 1 2 3 & 4 & 5 & 6 7 8)............................2 MEAS.

REPEAT FIRST TWO MEASURES AGAIN
only add STAMP ON LEFT FOOT. Ct. 8................2 MEAS.

BREAK:
Stamp forward on RIGHT foot, Step back on ball of LEFT, Stamp forward again on RIGHT foot, Shuffle LEFT ball change L. to R. Ankle turn on RIGHT to RIGHT, LUNGE on LEFT. (Ct. 1 2 3 & 4 & 5 6 7)............................2 MEAS.
                                                    8 MEAS.

Music Suggestion: "Stompin' at the Savoy"

GEORGE MURPHY STEP
(Soft Shoe Style)

Flap LEFT double shuffle R. ball change R. to L., flap on RIGHT (Ct. & 1 & a 2 & a 3 & 4)......................1 MEAS.

REPEAT TWO MORE TIMES...................................2 MEAS.

Shuffle LEFT, drop RIGHT heel, step back on ball of LEFT foot, flap forward RIGHT, flap forward LEFT (no weight). (Ct. & 1 & 2 & 3 & 4)...............................1 MEAS.

REPEAT FIRST THREE MEAS. Shuffle LEFT, drop RIGHT heel, step back on ball of LEFT foot, step to RIGHT AND ANKLE TURN RIGHT, LUNGE ON LEFT. (Ct. & 1 & 2 3 4)......................................4 MEAS.

8 MEAS.

Music Suggestion: "Tea For Two"

NICHOLAS BROTHERS STEP

Flap LEFT forward, hit tip of RIGHT toe, then heel of RIGHT foot (riff movement), drop LEFT heel, step across in front of LEFT on ball of RIGHT, drop RIGHT HEEL, LUNGE LEFT. (Ct. & 1 & a 2 & 3 4) ....1 MEAS.

REPEAT ON RIGHT, REPEAT AGAIN ON LEFT 2 MEAS.

Brush the RIGHT foot back, drop the LEFT heel, step back on RIGHT foot, LUNGE forward on LEFT, slide back on LEFT, at the same time raising the RIGHT leg with knee bent and STAMP on RIGHT forward.
(Ct. & a 1 2 3 4) ....1 MEAS.

REPEAT ALL .... 4 MEAS.

8 MEAS.

Music Suggestion: "Chattanooga Choo Choo"

SHIRLEY TEMPLE STEP
(Waltz Clog)

Flap LEFT, shuffle RIGHT, ball change R. to L.
(Ct. & 1 & 2 & 3) ....1 MEAS.

REPEAT ON RIGHT FOOT ....1 MEAS.

Stamp forward on LEFT, ball change R. to L., flap on
RIGHT (Ct. 1 & 2 & 3) ....1 MEAS.

Triple tap LEFT. Step on RIGHT. ANKLE TURN TO
RIGHT, Step LEFT (Ct. & 1 & 2 3) ....1 MEAS.

REPEAT ALL TO RIGHT. ....4 MEAS.

8 MEAS.

Music Suggestion: School Days or Missouri Waltz

Nick Castle's Dance Routine

ENTRANCE . . WAIT TWO MEASURES:

ENTER RIGHT. Walk in with swagger steps, R. L. R. L. Face front, fast ball change R. to L.
(Ct. 1 2 3 4 5 6 7 & a) ....2 MEAS.

STEP ONE

FLAP RIGHT, drop RIGHT heel, FLAP LEFT, drop LEFT HEEL, Flap RIGHT, Flap LEFT, then a RIGHT heel ROLL (4 heels) (Ct. & 1 2 & 3 4 & 5 & 6 & 7 & 8) ....2 MEAS.

REPEAT TWO MORE TIMES..............................4 MEAS.

BREAK:

Flap RIGHT, drop RIGHT heel two times.
Flap LEFT, drop LEFT heel two times.
Flap RIGHT, Shuffle L., Hop R., step back on LEFT (IRISH), Stamp on RIGHT.
(Ct. & 1 & 2 & 3 & 4 & 5 & a 6 & 7) ....2 MEAS.

8 MEAS.

STEP TWO

Flap LEFT, Shuffle RIGHT, ball change R. to L. STAMP on RIGHT. Flap LEFT, Shuffle RIGHT ball change R. to L. Then make an ANKLE TURN on LEFT to LEFT, STAMP

RIGHT. (Ct. & 1 & 2 & 3 4 & 5 & 6 & 7 8) ....2 MEAS.

REPEAT TWO MORE TIMES..............................4 MEAS.

BREAK:

Flap LEFT, Shuffle R. ball change R. to L. Flap RIGHT, Shuffle L., hop R., step back on LEFT (IRISH), STAMP RIGHT. Clap hands.
(Ct. & 1 & 2 & 3 & 4 & 5 & 6 7 8) ....2 MEAS.

8 MEAS.

STEP THREE

Step back on ball of LEFT foot, SCRAPE WITH RIGHT, drop LEFT heel, Flap RIGHT ball change L. to R. (right forward). Travel to LEFT WITH Flap L. ball change, ball change, ball change R. to L.
(Ct. 1 & 2 & 3 & 4 & 5 & 6 & 7 & 8) ....2 MEAS.

Flap forward on RIGHT, Flap forward on LEFT, CASTLE ROLL (see number 24) with RIGHT, Flap on RIGHT, CASTLE ROLL with LEFT, Flap on LEFT.
(Ct. & 1 & 2 & 3 & a 4 & 5 & 6 & a 7 & 8) ......2 MEAS.

Flap RIGHT ball change L. to R. LEFT CRAMP ROLL (see number 22). Single PEARL ROLL RIGHT. Single PEARL ROLL LEFT. (see number 25).
(Ct. & 1 & 2 & 3 & a 4 & 5 & 6 & a 7 & 8) ......2 MEAS.

BREAK:
Double PEARL ROLL on RIGHT, Double PEARL ROLL on LEFT.
Triple PEARL ROLL on RIGHT, Triple PEARL ROLL on LEFT.
(Ct. & 1 & a 2 & 3 & a 4 & a 5 & a 6
& a 7 & a 8) ....2 MEAS.
8 MEAS.

STEP FOUR

Flap on RIGHT, drop RIGHT heel, step back on ball of LEFT foot, brush the RIGHT back, drop LEFT heel, step back on RIGHT, step to side on ball of LEFT foot, shuffle RIGHT ball change R. to L. and make an ANKLE TURN on LEFT. Stamp on RIGHT. Clap hands.
(Ct. & 1 & 2 & a 3 4 & 5 & 6 7 8) ....2 MEAS.

REPEAT WITH LEFT FOOT......................................2 MEAS.

Step to RIGHT, drop RIGHT heel, step across in front of RIGHT with LEFT, making 1/2 turn to RIGHT, drop LEFT heel, swing the RIGHT foot to RIGHT side finishing with a stamp on RIGHT foot. (Three-Step-Turn to Right.)
(Ct. 1 & 2 & 3 hold 4) ....1 MEAS.

REPEAT THIS LAST MEASURE TO LEFT..............1 MEAS.

BREAK:
Stamp forward on RIGHT.
Stamp forward on LEFT.
Toe tap the RIGHT in back, drop LEFT heel making 1/4 turn LEFT, Stamp on RIGHT, brush the LEFT back, drop RIGHT heel, Stamp on LEFT, ball change R. to L. completing 1/2 pivot to LEFT. Face front finishing with STAMP on RIGHT foot.
(Ct. 1 2 & 3 & 4 & 5 & 6 7) ....2 MEAS.
8 MEAS.

CARMEN MIRANDA STEP
(Samba Boogie Tap)

Step forward on ball of LEFT foot, ball change R. L. (right in back). (Ct. 1 & 2.) Flap forward on RIGHT foot, ball change L. to R. (right forward.) (& 3 & 4)..........1 MEAS.

LUNGE on LEFT, clap hands overhead, LUNGE ON RIGHT, clap hands overhead. (Ct. 5 6 7 8) (On lunge LEFT, left hip out to side, on lunge RIGHT, right hip out to side.
1 MEAS.

MOVE TO LEFT ON FOLLOWING. Step LEFT to side (digging ball of foot), clap hands, cross RIGHT over LEFT, clap hands, dig step LEFT to side, ball change R. to L. Clap hands. (Ct. 1 & 2 & 3 & a 4)...................1 MEAS.

REPEAT THIS MOVEMENT MOVING TO RIGHT 1 MEAS.

REPEAT ALL ....4 MEAS.

8 MEAS.

Music Suggestion: "Tico Tico" or "Brazil"

CPSIA information can be obtained
at www.ICGtesting.com
Printed in the USA
LVHW090510230919
631935LV00009B/111/P